SURVIVAL HINTS

ALLIED AIR FORCES.
DIRECTORATE OF INTELLIGENCE,
S.W.P.A.

RESTRICTED

SURVIVAL HINTS

ALLIED AIR FORCES
DIRECTORATE OF INTELLIGENCE
S.W.P.A.

1943

SOA Books

SURVIVAL HINTS

This Edition Copyright
© 2013 by SOA Books

Cover, Layout and Graphics by: SOA Books

ISBN-13:
978-1484112830

ISBN-10:
1484112830

Printed in U.S.A

Introduction

SINCE the war began, many hundreds of pilots and crewmen who have been force-landed in uncivilized areas of the Southwest Pacific, have made their way back to friendly territory . . . . some with the benefit of complete survival kits . . . . others with no more than a few pieces of equipment, plus resourcefulness and a determination to return to their base.

This booklet is designed to give you a few helpful hints on survival in the jungle, at sea, or on low, sandy islands. It is printed in water-proof ink on water-proof paper and was especially prepared for easy reference by you.

Perhaps you will wonder why this booklet will seem to be concerned mainly with the New Guinea Jungle. This has been done designedly. The New Guinea Jungle is the most difficult terrain in which to live and make your way: other areas in this theatre will be easier; if you can conquer the former, the latter should cause you little trouble; and what you are told in this booklet about New Guinea will be equally valuable elsewhere.

CLOTHING and EQUIPMENT

Do not handicap your chances of survival by being improperly outfitted ! The following is a check-list of the outer clothing and equipment you should carry on every mission :

LONG-SLEEVED SHIRT AND TROUSERS : The 8.2 Chino material is best suited for jungle wear. Shorts must never be worn.

LEATHER FLYING JACKET : It is strongly recommended, and will be much appreciated if it is necessary to spend much time in the mountains, where the nights are cold.

SOCKS, SERVICE : Two pairs of service socks, of wool and cotton mixture, will protect your feet, absorb perspiration, last longer, protect your ankles from mosquitoes, and when pulled up over the bottom of your trousers, will protect your legs from leeches. Upon a forced-landing, one pair should be removed and socks washed and changed daily.

4

SHOES, SERVICE : Either GI service shoes or paratroop boots. Never wear the fleece-lined flying boots, for they come apart easily when saturated with water, and thus make ill-fitting, uncomfortable footwear, which will cause blisters. Also, never wear low-cut shoes, cloth-lined boots or shoes, cheap shoes, new shoes, or worn-out shoes.

SURVIVIAL ACCESSORIES TO BE CARRIED ON ALL MISSIONS

PARACHUTE : The parachute, if you are able to retrieve it, will serve many purposes : the straps can be split and used for pack straps and leggings, to protect the legs from leeches and insects; the canopy will provide a tent, a sleeping bag, a hammock, a towel, a poncho; the shroud lines may be used for tent ropes, fishing lines, tourniquets, etc.

MAE WEST : This may also be used as a water container, when on land. Before the take-off, check the condition of the CO_2 bottles and make certain they are properly filled and unpunctured.

MIRROR : A metal mirror should be carried in the breast pocket, for it should be on your person in case of a bail-out, where it might be necessary to free yourself of the parachute and its kit. The mirror is most essential for signalling, particularly if you are in the water.

HEAVY LEATHER GLOVES : These are needed to protect hands against cuts and scratches, and possible resultant infections. They should be carried in a trouser pocket.

BURNING GLASS—MATCHES : The blue-headed wax "Vesta" matches, in waterproof box, are recommended. Both the glass and the matches should be carried in the pocket.

HEAD NET : An essential in the jungle.

THE MACHETE : Can be conveniently carried in a case, strapped to the lower leg. In this position, it gives added protection against skinning the shins, and other possible injury to the leg. Also, in this position, it is convenient to get at, if your 'chute is caught in a tree !

.45 PISTOL—EXTRA AMMUNITION :

- If the pistol holster has a loop for belt attachment, insert the web belt, as otherwise the snap, when the 'chute opens, may cause the eyelets to tear out.
- Make certain the holster flap is securely buttoned.
- A lanyard should be added for fastening pistol holster to the leg.
- If wearing a shoulder holster, see that it is properly adjusted under the armpit, and free of the 'chute straps. The snap of the 'chute is sufficient to cause a broken rib.

- The pistol should be heavily greased as a precaution against sea-water.

- .45 shells filled with No. 7 shot will increase the value of gun. Do not carry lead ball ammunition.

CANTEEN WITH CUP : These items should be atached to the web belt.

HUNTING KNIFE IN SHEATH : This should be attached to the web belt. A sharpening stone should also be added, If possible.

DRYING RACK

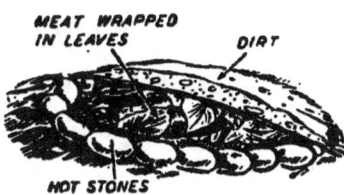

MEAT WRAPPED IN LEAVES   DIRT

HOT STONES

ROASTING PIT

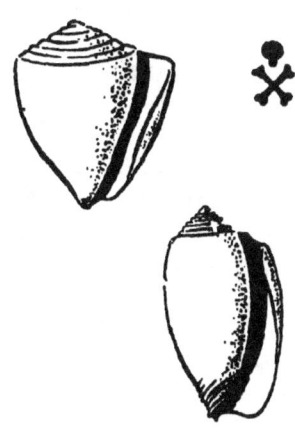

CONES - SEASNAILS DANGEROUS

7

II

The Crash-Landing or the Bail-Out

THERE are a number of important advantages to be gained by a crash-landing, rather than a bail-out, in friendly territory. These are as follows:—

RADIO EQUIPMENT : It may be preserved for use in contacting the searching parties.

ADDITIONAL SUPPLIES : These are available in the plane.

SHELTER : The plane will provide shelter until such time as the crew members will have become oriented to ground conditions, or have been located by searching parties, or have organized plans for moving on.

SURVIVAL : The problems of survival, and those of aiding the injured, can better be faced by the crew as a functional unit.

SALVAGE : The plane has salvage value.

TERRAIN SUITABLE FOR CRASH-LANDING

. A successful crash-landing depends upon the availability of suitable terrain. When you have decided on the area in which you will make your crash-landing, endeavour to radio your position before landing. The crash may wreck your radio.

FORWARD FIELDS AND EMERGENCY AREAS : Previously examined and found satisfactory for this purpose. (They are usually kunai grass-covered flat areas). In the upper SEPIK RIVER, there are large grassy areas suitable for normal landings. AVOID those on which there are sinuous strips of another shade of green, as these strips are probably paralleling a drainage course.

OLD RIVER TERRACES : Obstacles to landing are a few scattered trees and stumps hidden by the grass. The surfaces are usually well drained and dry. Often, there is a series of ditches cutting the surface, several feet in depth and width, which constitute the drainage pattern. These old terraces are recognised as flat strips of land in the valleys, into which the stream has cut a channel.

LARGE RIVER SAND-BARS : Obstacles may be partially buried tree trunks, stumps, low-scrub-bush, and possible flood conditions.   .

RIVER FLOOD PLAINS OR PARTIALLY FILLED-IN LAKES : Obstacles here are presented by the soil, which will be very soft because it is little more than a mass of mud and humus.

NIPA PALM AREAS : These areas will be found extensively in the great swamps and along the lower courses of the large rivers, particularly in New Guinea. They are recognisable from the air by their velvet-like, smooth surface. Successful crash-landings have been made in this growth.

PROCEDURE UPON CRASH-LANDING

As soon as you have landed in friendly territory, the first objective is to aid the searching planes. Stay with your plane for several days, as rescue contact may be by friendly natives or patrols on foot, who have learned of your position. You should do the following :

RADIO YOUR POSITION : Providing your radio is functioning. ' S.O.S. messages may be sent 15 minutes before and after the hour.

MAKE SIGNALLING PREPARATIONS : Searching planes may possibly come over the area immediately. They certainly will be over at sunrise and at noon the following two days. You should, if possible:—

- Gather a large pile of firewood.

- Light it and keep it going.
- Drain oil from the engines and store it in containers near the firewood, along with containers of water.
- Outline your plane to eliminate the effect of its camouflage. You can do this in several ways : Cut away branches over-hanging the plane. Spread your orange-colored life rafts, Mae Wests, and ponchos over the plane. They will present the maximum contrast to the jungle colors. Drape your parachutes over the wing tips and tail. Remove the engine cowlings and place them upside down on the wings, using as reflectors.

WHEN SEARCH PLANES APPROACH :

- Build up the fire.
- Pour alternately on to the fire, oil (to make black smoke), and water (to make white steam).
- Signal planes with mirror, flares or other available signalling devices.

PROCEDURE BEFORE BAILING OUT

If you are unable to find suitable terrain for a crash-landing, or, if for any other reason, you must bail out, there are some things which you should try to do before you leave your ship.

RADIO YOUR POSITION IF POSSIBLE.

ADJUST EQUIPMENT : Fasten your jungle kit, machete or jungle knife, and your other equipment securely on your person. If wearing a shoulder holster, adjust the pistol under the armpit in a manner that.the jerk on the straps will not cause a broken rib. Bailout, if possible, over a grass-covered area to minimize the risk of bodily injury upon landing.

SELECT YOUR LANDING SPOT : Do not bail out in an area where you might land in a lake. Lakes are usually infested with crocodiles. Do not attempt to attract the natives' attention by flying low and firing machine gun bursts over their village. This action may scare away the more primitive natives. If there are natives in this area, they will have heard you miles away, and in all probability, they will see your 'chutes as you descend.

THE BAIL-OUT

CREWS : The air crews should attempt to bail out in pairs. They should plan to rendezvous with those who are in the direction of the nearest base. When the two members of a pair have joined, they should wait until all the pairs who first bailed out have moved up to join them. In other words, the second pair will await the first, and then the two pairs will move up together to join the third. The last pair to bail out will remain where they landed until all others have joined them or will have been accounted for. Where, after the crew had bailed out, the plane was seen to crash without burning, all crew members should make for the plane as their place of rendezvous and proceed as outlined in "Procedure Upon Crash-Landing".

STUDY TERRAIN AS YOU DESCEND :

- Fix the location of the drained ground with reference to the swampy areas.
- Look for clearings in the jungle—they may be native gardens or villages. (In some parts of Dutch New Guinea, the natives in the limestone areas build their homes on or near the tops of the limestone pinnacles. There may be several acres of fairly flat land around the houses).

PLANE : Watch where your plane falls, and also where the other members of the crew land.

DESCENT IN HEAVY TIMBER :

- Keep your legs and feet together, knees slightly bent.

- Protect your ribs by keeping your arms close to your chest.
- Keep your hands, palms inward, over your face.
- Do not look down. Inclining your head forward may result in a broken nose, or broken neck, when you hit the trees.

PROCEDURE UPON LANDING

SHOCK : Should you be suffering from shock, take a benzedrine tablet from your kit.

PARACHUTE : Try to retrieve your parachute; it will serve a multitude of purposes, as previously mentioned.

COVER : Protect such things as will be be harmed by rain or dampness. Wrap your watch, compass and pistol in oilskin, or in the silk from a panel of your 'chute.

SHOES : Attach brass hobnails (screws), or cricket spikes to your shoes, (twelve in each sole, six in each heel), and save the balance in case some pull out while travelling. If they pull out, pack moss into the holes and replace them.

WATER : Locate water, purify it, and store some away.

- When searching for water, mark the trail well so that you will be able to return to your original position.

- Purify the water, either by boiling or by the use of halazone tablets or iodine drops. Use 1 Halazone tablet for each quart of water, shake a container and leave half an hour, then shake again before using. Do not use stagnant water unless there are no other sources.

- Rainwater can be caught in the panels of the 'chute or on leaves.

- Extra water can be stored in bamboo tubes, or in one or both lungs of the Mae West.

IF YOU HAVE LANDED IN A SWAMP

Your procedure is determined by the time of day with reference to the time it will require to retrieve your 'chute and to build a camp, either in the swamp, or, having walked out of the swamp, on the drained land. In the swamps, the mosquitoes come out in force about 1700 hours (about an hour before darkness).

IF BEFORE 1400 HOURS :

- Try to retrieve ALL of your parachute. This should not be difficult since the vegetation is mainly soft, pithy wood, and is easily cut and handled. Then work your way out of the swamp to the drained land.

IF AFTER 1400 HOURS, AND YOU ARE A GOOD DISTANCE FROM DRAINED LAND :

- Make camp at once. You will need a bed above the water and the mud. Tie poles between trees; surface these with shorter ones tied crosswise to form the bed-platform. A bed or hammock can be made from lengths of rattan vine slung between trees. During the night your body will be protected from the mosquitoes by your clothing, gloves, socks and head-net. The wrists and ankles may be protected further by making putties of large leaves.

- Cover the bed by making a lean-to covered with large leaves.

- After the bed has been prepared, retrieve your parachute if possible.

- The next morning, make your way out to the drained land.

- When you have reached the drained land, build smoke signals to attract the other members of your crew, and wait for them.

CRASH-LANDING ON A RIVER SAND-BAR

If your plane has been crash-landed on a river sand-bar, some of the problems of overland travel through the jungle may be eliminated. And if you are in New Guinea and the streams flow toward the south coast, your subsequent journey may not be too difficult.

Large sand-bars suitable for crash-landings are generally found in large rivers, bordered by wide swamp areas. The best way to travel will be downstream by raft.

Remain near your plane for several days and until hope of being located by searching planes has been abandoned. Then prepare to leave the area.

BUILD RAFT : Build one or more large rafts, depending upon the size of your party. See Section IV. Use rubber life rafts as well, but you must exercise caution in order to keep them from being snagged by the rocks and sunken branches hidden under the sluggish, muddy waters.

SALVAGE SUPPLIES : Before leaving the plane, salvage all supplies you can transport.

FRAME FOR BED   LOG REFLECTOR

III

Natives and Obtaining Native Aid

IN territory not under Japanese control, it is very difficult to predict the type of natives that you will encounter, or their reaction and attitude towards you when passing through their territory. The further inland you are, in the uncontrolled mountainous interior, the more difficult it becomes to make any predictions.

The term "uncontrolled area" means those localities where in the past, natives were contacted only occasionally by a government patrol, or they may never have seen a white man. The inhabitants of such areas live now as they have for many generations, carrying on their tribal customs, unimpressed by the world outside.

The natives may or may not fear the white man. How they react to your presence will be determined to a great extent by their degree of fear. Because this will vary between localities not far removed from each other, one party may make a successful contact with the natives, while the next party only a short distance away, may not see one native.

INLAND TRIBES

. Some of the inland tribes and those inhabiting the mountainous, coastal areas, are remnants of tribes who were forced to retire into the hills by incoming tribes who were more powerful. Those who did not retire to hills were either assimilated or annihilated by the new arrivals. And those who did go back into the hills sometimes were able to hold their own under the more difficult living conditions, while others degenerated or even died out entirely.

These tribal stocks vary greatly, from pigmoids who, incidentally, are usually friendly, to very large physical types; from negroids to light-skinned types. The light-colored skin and large physique probably indicate a mixture with Polynesian stock.

The mountain tribes are generally hostile to the coastal people, and they may or may not be hostile to their neighbours in the mountains. In the past, they occasionally raided the coastal area, often killing whole communities and burning villages. The coastal natives fear these people, and will not venture beyond their own boundaries.

The coastal tribes, in turn, may be hostile to one another. Much of their misunderstandings undoubtedly result from the confusion of dialects.

DIALECTS VARY

This wide variety of dialects has developed in part from the native habit of isolation of individual groups in certain definite areas which are enclosed by distinct topographical boundaries. People from one area seldom venture into another. For example, in the great swamp lands along the south coast of New Guinea, one tribe may consider its area to be bounded on either side by a large stream. In the alluvial plains near the coast, two large rivers or watersheds or one or more streams may mark the extent of the tribe's country. Where the mountains reach all the way down to the sea, a tribe may be confined within a single narrow valley. This will also be true of much of the mountainous interior of New Guinea.

This separation and isolation of the tribes within the friendly areas will make it clear to you why it is so difficult to predict what your reception will be from the natives in any particular locality.

YOUR CONTACT WITH THE NATIVES

If there are natives in the vicinity, and they are not afraid, they will locate you within a few hours provided it is not too late in the afternoon. If it is late, they will probably arrive a few hours after sunrise the next morning. They will help you retrieve your parachutes, build signal fires and shelters, serve as your guides, and do a multitude of different chores for you. You can pay for their services with such trade items as tobacco, salt tablets, razor blades, silk from your parachutes for lap-laps, beads, etc.

If you have observed smokes in the vicinity and yet no natives have contacted you before noon on the day after you landed, you can safely conclude that the natives are either too shy to contact you, or are indifferent to your presence. Then you must make steps to contact them.

- Don't waste time by attempting to reach a smoke unless you have observed it in the same location for several days. A single small smoke of short duration will probably have been made by wandering natives who have passed on by the time you reach it.

- Make smokes of your own by day and fires by night.

- Make smokes in or near the natives' garden areas.

- You can make a drum-like noise, audible for miles, by beating the buttress-like roots of trees with a club.

- If you come to a deserted village merely wait for the natives to approach you, even if necessary to wait several hours.

THE INDIRECT APPROACH

Because of the fear of the white man which many of the natives possess, the indirect contact may be your only method of winning their aid.

If a native garden is discovered, several members of the party should visit it for food. They should take only a small quantity of food away, and they should leave a payment of a razor blade, a needle, or a twist of tobacco, placed on a stick in the centre of the garden where it can be readily seen.

This may be the first contact these shy people have ever had with the white man. So make it good; it will help you and those who may find themselves in a similar situation at a later date.

You may never see the owner of the garden, but the fact that you have treated him fairly will precede you to his village. In all probability, the natives will then contact you somewhere along your route. They may not lead you to their villages, but they will put you on the right trails leading out of their country and provide you with food, either as a gift or a trade.

If these attempts at direct and indirect contact with the natives have been unsuccessful, do not waste any more time or energy, for it is most difficult to contact them if they do not wish to meet you. You may

22

even wander into a native village, but, if the natives don't wish to see you, they will simply abandon their village and hide for as long as you are in the neighborhood.

NATIVE GUIDES

If native aid is obtained, you must not expect the native guides to go more than a few days' walk from their villages. At the end of that time they will have reached the boundary of their country, a point beyond which they will usually refuse to go. Even were they to go on, they would be of little value to you for they would be afraid and would not be familiar with the territory. It may then be several days before you could make contact with the tribe in the new locality.

HOSTILE NATIVES

If you have made no native contacts, you must keep an eye open for warning signs of the belligerency of the natives. Those who are afraid of the white man may indicate their displeasure with your presence by placing obstacles along the trails to indicate that they do not want trespassers in their country.

Where acts of belligerency have occurred, or where, after hostile warnings, you have been unable to win the natives over to you, it would be wise for you to retrace your steps and go around the area. This will require at the most only a few days' delay. If the boundary is a watershed, go either to the right or left, working your way in the general direction of your base.

CURRENCIES, TRADE ITEMS AND RATES OF EXCHANGE

When dealing with natives, remember that it is best not to over-pay them. Ration out your money or trade items. In the coastal areas, where the natives have had greater contact with the white man, money and medicines are acceptable. Silver money is especially prized if it is bright and shiny.

TRADE GOODS

When money is not acceptable, or you do not have any with you, trade items are the normal means of exchange : native leaf tobacco, strong knives, axe heads, fish hooks, needles, beads, and razor blades, are the more popular "trade goods." All good iron and steel tools are especially welcomed. In the interior, where the natives are more primitive, salt, beads and razor blades are much coveted. In the Wissel Lakes area of New Guinea, cowrie shells serve as currency and are highly valued.

TRADING VALUE

.The trading value of some of these items may be seen from the following examples:—To be the owner of a steel axe head is a native's highest ambition. If he once has one, however, don't expect to get any more work out of him. An axe head should be given only in payment for a canoe or for work over an extended period—it is too valuable to give for anything less. Knives belong in the same category as axe heads. The owner of a pandanus tree cut down by mistake was considered amply reimbursed by one cowrie shell. In the Wissel Lakes area, the price of a pig is 40 cowrie shells.

If you have neither money nor trade items, you can pay by giving a "paper"—a writing in which you state that you were helped by the native bearer of the paper, and that he should be rewarded suitably. Sign it with your name, rank and serial number. It will be honored by the proper authorities.

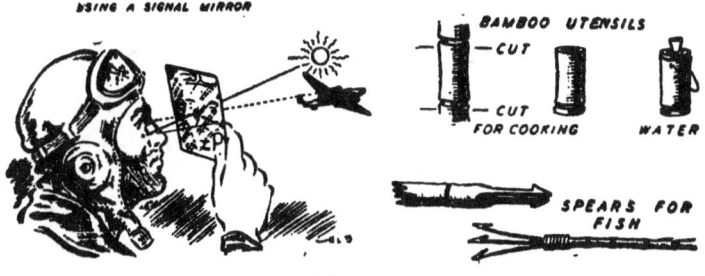

USING A SIGNAL MIRROR

BAMBOO UTENSILS

—CUT

—CUT
FOR COOKING

WATER

SPEARS FOR
FISH

IV.

Travelling in the Jungles

GENERAL COMMENT

TRAVELLING through the jungles is not easy; it is tiresome to cut trails and wade through mud, or continuously to be climbing up and down slippery ledges and over moss-covered rocks.

The direction of your travel is determined by a number of factors : the topography, the direction of your base, the location of the enemy in relation to the place where you find yourself.

HINTS ON JUNGLE TRAVEL

DO NOT HURRY :   Haste means exhaustion.

REST :   Get plenty of rest at night; the pains you take with your camping preparations will pay big dividends.   See Section V.

SHELTER :   Keep out of the rain at night by building a lean-to of poles and leaves to shed the rain.

DIRECTION : Always keep compass notes of your travel (direction and time), or you may find yourself going in circles for days.

TRAILS : When you find a trail, use all your powers of concentration to follow it:—

- Most trails, from the white man's point of view, are very narrow, muddy, and poorly marked.

- No trails exist without reason. Each one leads somewhere. If you come to an intersection, follow the main trail, provided, of course, that it is going in the right direction.

- Native trails usually follow ridges or stream valleys. In the latter case, if the stream is swift, the valley will be narrow and the trail will cross and re-cross it. If the stream is small and sluggish, the trail will generally follow the bank near the edge where the ground is dry.

CUTTING TRAILS : If you must cut your own trail, cut only that which is necessary. Do not waste your energy trying to cut through dense bush, kunai grass or swamp growth. Push around it. If for any reason you intend to return to the point you are leaving, be sure to blaze your trail clearly.

STREAMS : If you come to streams, do not swim them unless absolutely necessary. If you must swim a stream, first go upstream from the point which you wish to reach on the opposite bank, and then swim diagonally downstream with the current. It is a good plan to use the buoyancy of a log to help you. Take a dry pole or a bamboo about nine feet long and three inches in diameter; hold it between your knees with the forward end out of the water. Another method is to fell a tree across a stream, if possible. Avoid swimming large streams in the evenings, as this is the time when the crocodiles are feeding.

TOPOGRAPHIC FEATURES OF THE TERRAIN

All flying personnel should familiarize themselves with the various types of terrains and the living conditions related to each type. A study of aerial photographs is an excellent manner of learning the general topographic features of each of the six types of terrain. Such study should be continued to the point where you can recognise these features instantly, because the cloud conditions in the tropics are such that you may not have more than a moment's clear view. You must be able to distinguish from the air:—

- The boundary between dry land and swamps.
- The boundary between the piedmont and the mountains.

- Stream patterns and the types of terrain indicated by these patterns and the associated vegetation.

TYPES OF TERRAIN

What you should do and the direction in which you should travel is determined to a great extent by the terrain. The following are descriptions of the various types of terrains, suggested methods of movements through them, and some general remarks on the possibilities of subsistence in each:—

MOUNTAINS : In travelling through the mountrains, you should follow either the stream courses or the ridges, preferably the latter—and particularly if they are grass-covered and out of sight of Japanese outposts.

- Do not try to travel along the slopes half-way up the sides of the valleys; this will only take you into tributary valleys from which you will have to retrace your steps.

- Do not attempt to travel down these mountain streams by canoe or raft; there are too many rapids and waterfalls.

- Determine your general compass direction of travel from your map. Then choose the stream or ridge route which corresponds to that bearing. Both streams and ridges will follow sinuous courses, but the over-all direction will be shown on the map and the proper route may be selected.

- You will have little hope of contacting natives in the mountainous areas. They are few, and are afraid of strangers.

- Nights in the higher altitudes are cold. Build shelters and use your parachute panels or flying jacket for cover.

- WATER from the mountain streams will be clear, cold and good. If you are travelling along the ridge route, you will have to obtain your water from vines or bamboos with moss on them, along the trail, or from rain water which you have caught in your 'chute. So if you take the ridge route, you may choose to carry water which you have obtained from the stream lower down.

- FOOD in this area is very scarce. There are ferns, rattan vines, a few tree frogs and birds.

PLATEAU AREAS

The majority of the plateau-type topography represents uplifted coralline reefs, and is composed of limestones. Since the time of their uplifting, they have been dissected by surface and sub-surface stream drainage! The rocks have been weathered by rain water to form a very rough pitted surface with innumerable sharp points jutting out to cut or tear the flesh if you slip and fall.

Travel across these plateaux is most difficult in the absence of a trail. There are numerous small sink-holes and caverns covered by decayed vegetation which will not support the weight of a man.

The trails that exist all pass through the saddles between the conical-shaped pinnacles.

- Work your way through the saddles between the pinnacles, but adhere strictly to the predetermined compass direction in your effort to find a trail.

- Once or twice each day, climb a pinnacle and observe the surrounding terrain for native gardens or trails.

- When you locate a trail, it will lead you to a native garden or a village.

- If the trail forks, take the main branch, or, if each seems equal, take the one which conforms to your general compass direction.

- WATER in this area will be good but scarce, since most of the drainage is subterranean. Thus you may have to resort to water-vines or to catching rain water.

- FOOD may be obtained from the few natives, or from the scattered native gardens that may be found.

ALLUVIAL PLAINS

This terrain is characterised by relatively flat land extending coastward from the foothills. There are usually swamps separating it from the beach.

Travel is easiest in this type of terrain, for it has a gentle slope and there are but few rough places.

When you have reached this alluvial plain region, you may turn right or left from the general compass course and proceed until you reach a large stream. Then, either build a raft or walk down the bank of the stream until you reach a native village—generally, it will be no more than one day's walk. At the village you will probably have little trouble in obtaining a canoe and paddlers. The existence of numerous native villages and gardens makes contact with the natives quite easy.

RAFTING : In the upper Alluvial Plains, in the sections bordering the foothills, rafting is not advisable. The streams are too swift and their continuous flooding has resulted in numerous sand-bars and gravel-bars being formed in the upper reaches. If rafting should be done in swiftly flowing waters, you must be on the alert at all times for the roar of rapids and water-falls, and be prepared to abandon the raft.

CONSTRUCTION OF RAFT : Suitable wood can usually be found along the stream courses. Much of the jungle wood is too hard and lacks buoyancy, so either have the natives aid you in selecting the wood, or choose dead wood, which generally will float. If logs aren't available, you can cut bamboo poles, tie them together into a bundle and use four or five bundles in the place of that many logs. Tie the logs (or the bundles) together in at least three or four places with shroud lines from your 'chute or rattan vines. Generally, your raft should be about 6 feet wide by 10 feet long for one man, and correspondingly larger for more. Construct a paddle from a piece of wood about three feet long and about three inches in diameter. Split this log down the middle and fashion yourself a handle at one end.

TRAVEL VIA RAFT : Tie a 30 foot length of rattan vine to one end of the raft. Keep it coiled and readily accessible in case it becomes necessary for you to jump off the raft. Should that happen, grab the end of the coil and make for shore—you may be able to prevent the loss of your raft and equipment. Tie all your equipment securely on board. Carry enough water with you to see you through the brackish water conditions which exist along the lower portions of the larger streams. Bamboo tubes or coconuts can be used for canteens. If coconuts are available, a double bunch of five should be tied together with a two foot length of rattan vine. In such form they can serve as emergency life preservers (water wings) should the need arise.

WATER is readily obtainable from the numerous streams. Near the mouths of the streams it is brackish and contaminated with the tidal water, but this, in limited amounts, is not injurious.

FOOD : Relatively, there is an abundance of food in this area. Practically all of the meats and vegetables mentioned in Section VI. can be found here. The native gardens is the source of most of the vegetables.

SWAMP AREAS

The great swamp areas which exist between the alluvial plains and the coastal areas, are extremely difficult terrain to traverse on foot. A raft or canoe offers the best medium of travel through the mangrove swamps. Dead mangrove logs can be used.

- In the lower courses of the streams, rafting can only be successfully accomplished during the two daily periods following high tide conditions.

- Keep the raft at all times in the stream channel with the use of your pole or paddle. Should you get out of the channel and drift into an ox-bow lake in the lower reaches of the stream, you might find it impossible to get out of this water and back into the stream channel.

- There are also swamps in some of the river valleys contained between natural levees and the foot-hills, that have been built up as part of the stream bank through years of flooding. Rarely do these river swamp areas have a width of more than four or five miles. There will be cut-offs and ox-bow lakes meandering through these swamps as the result of the changes in the river courses, following their flooding. The water is stagnant fresh water, except near the mouths of the rivers, where it becomes brackish as the result of the tidal effect. The presence of mangrove and nipa nipa palms will indicate the point where the streams become brackish. In these river swamp areas, the best place to travel on foot is along the river bank, but, at the first opportunity a raft should be built and used to take you to the river's mouth.

- The lower courses of the larger streams (New Guinea in particular), are tidal for 20 to 30 miles inland; whether and where it becomes tidal can be determined by the presence of mangrove trees and nipa palms along the shore. In these tidal sections you must tie up your raft at the shore during the incoming tides, or it will be carried back up the river. As you get closer to the mouths, your precautions must be greater. Use several heavy vines with which to moor the raft, and wedge it as well by implanting some poles in the mud. Then you yourself should get up on the bank before the tidal bore sweeps you away. It is sometimes four feet high, and rolls in with considerable force.

STRAND AND THE ASSOCIATED BEACH

- Travel through this area may be either by boat (obtainable from the natives), or on foot. Villages along the coast are seldom more than a day's walk apart.

- Crossing the mouths of large streams should be done by raft or canoe. If by raft, the crossing should be started when the tide is almost full, for a falling tide may sweep the raft out to sea or on to the sand-bar across the mouth; a rising tide may carry it far upstream. You can check the condition of the tide by observing the high water mark on the beach.

- Small streams may be crossed on foot at low tide by walking across the sand-bar at the mouth, but be extremely cautious, for this is a favourite place for crocodiles.

- WATER will be difficult to find if there is a mangrove swamp behind the strand. One course is to dig a hole in the sand just above the high tide mark. As soon as the water begins to seep in, stop digging and let the hole fill up. Seepage time will be about half an hour. While waiting, whittle a spoon from a piece of dry wood. There will be on top of this seepage a layer of about half an inch of fresh water. Skim this off carefully with the spoon, being careful not to disturb and mix the layers of water. This top layer will be slightly brackish, but usable. Augment this supply of water with coconut milk, clam juice, water obtained from water vines, or from the juice wrung out of diced fish flesh.

- SEA FOOD is abundant, but meats are scarce. Bananas, pandanus nuts, coconuts and other fruits and vegetables are available from native gardens.

V.

Camping in the Jungle

BECAUSE of the mosquitoes and rain, the necessity of preserving your strength, the arrangements you make for camping and sleeping in the jungle are of importance.

TIME TO MAKE CAMP

Early night-fall (1800 to 1820 hours), and the coming of the mosquitoes (approximately 1700 hours), make it imperative that you break off your travel by 1630 hours if you are to have sufficient time and light to make your camp. In the mountains, the afternoon rains start about 1530 hours.

CHOICE OF SITE

- Choose well-drained land if possible.
- Do not make your camp on the low, muddy banks of small streams (if it rains heavily that night your camp will be flooded).

35

- Do not make camp under trees with dead limbs or under coconut palms. Falling branches or nuts broken off by the storm can cause you serious injury.

- The natural levees which form the banks of large rivers are satisfactory sites, because they are relatively the highest points in the vicinity.

- If there are indications of the presence of crocodiles along the banks of the stream, make yourself a bed-platform by tying poles between trees at least 6 or 8 feet above ground. Brace the poles so they will not slip down during the night.

PREPARATION OF SITE

- Clean out all undergrowth around the immediate camp site.

- Build a good fire against an old log. The fire may be started by using shavings, moss or dry twigs. Dead wood lying on the ground may be wet through, but if you strip the bark from standing dead wood it will burn well.

39

TENT

You can construct a moderately water-proof tent out of the panels of your parachute canopy. (See Sketch.) A lean-to shelter may also be made with forked sticks and large leaves.

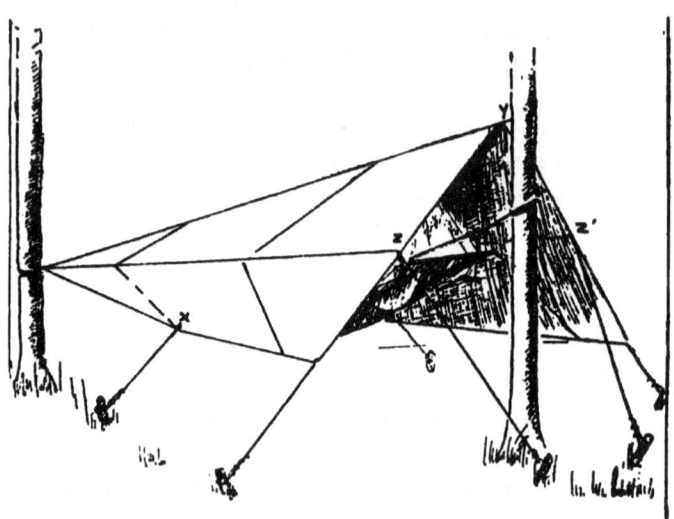

MAKING A TENT FROM THE PARACHUTE

To provide yourself an excellent tent, cut a four-panel slice from the parachute. Cut on the outside of the seams and cut the far end of the shroud lines so as to leave the lines as long as possible. Giving the panels a number, you will have used panels 1-6 for the hammock; use panel 7 as a waste panel by cutting on the inside of its seams, and make the tent out of panels 8, 9, 10 and 11.

In order to provide side tent lines, puncture a hole large enough to insert a shroud line at the strongest point of intersection of the seams (X) as shown on the drawing. Make the hole on the inside of the shroud line within the seam; insert a short line and tie it.

In erecting the tent, first put up the hammock. Then tie the middle line (Y) to the tree holding the head of the hammock; tie the tent close to the tree, in order to cover the head well, and several feet above the hammock. Tie all five lines at the apex of the panels to the other tree and considerably lower down. Pull these lines quite taut—the entire surface of the tent should be smooth and taut, so as to shed water better. Make six tent pins, drive them in at proper spots and tie the tent lines to them. Use the two lines (Z to Z') or not, as you see fit. Pin the mosquito canopy to the ridge of the tent above your face. You then have an excellent sleeping arrangement which is off the ground.

MAKING A HAMMOCK FROM THE PARACHUTE

Cut a six panel slice from the parachute : cut on the outside of the seams and leave shroud lines as long as possible. Fold over four panels so that the hammock has four panels in thickness. The remaining two panels are for cover. Erect the hammock between trees about 15 feet apart. This hammock will be longer than necessary, and if placed under the tent described above would catch rain water. To prevent this, tie the narrow foot-end of the hammock into a knot, thus shortening it by several inches. Then proceed to make tent covering as indicated by sketch.

SLEEPING BAG

Other panels of your 'chute canopy can be used for a sleeping bag. Take three of the panels and cut them about $2\frac{1}{2}$ yards from the peripheral seam. Fold the ends lengthwise and pin together the small ends and the sides. Cut an 18 inch piece away from the top panel as an opening for your face and attach your mosquito net over this opening. Tie the centre of the net to a stick so as to raise it from your face. Such a sleeping bag will give you warmth and protection from the rain and mosquitoes.

GROUND SHEET

The apron of the rubber dinghy will provide you with a good light-weight ground sheet, which may also be used as a protection against rain and cold.

BATHING, WASHING AND DRYING CLOTHES

- The presence of crocodiles makes bathing hazardous in slow-running waters. Instead of getting into the stream, dip the water out in a bamboo tube or cup and pour it over your body. And always have a way of retreat up the bank in case crocodiles come for you.

- Never wash your clothes in the evening. That is the time the mosquitoes are out in force.

- Air-dry shoes and other leather goods. If you put them in front of a fire the leather might be burned or dry too fast, harden and crack, leaving you barefoot.

CARE OF FEET

Your feet deserve and must have the best possible care if they are going to take you back to civilization. Wash them carefully every evening, and dry them well at all times. As often as possible when travelling, remove your shoes and socks and expose your feet to the air and sun, but do not sunburn. At the first sign of a blister, scratch or sore spot, stop at once, apply Antiseptic (not Iodine), and cover with adhesive plaster. Let the plaster take the wear instead of your skin.

FIRE

Building a fire in the jungles is of the utmost importance. They can be kindled in spite of the continuous downpour of rain and apparent wetness of everything about. First, one must build a lean-to shelter which will shelter the person as well as the preparations. Then get some dead wood from branches of a fallen tree; whittle off the wet outside portion; then shave the firm dry wood. From a pile of shavings, one should ordinarily get a fire started with a single match. Firm (not rotten) twigs, will start quickly if placed in wigwam style over the flame. These will stay in place, merely by sticking them into the soft soil.

PRESERVATION OF FIRE

Since fire is a necessity in the jungle, you may have to carry it along with you if you are out of matches, have no burning-glass or are unable to make a fire with friction. Make a piece of punk by cutting the outside off a piece of dead wood, and firing it. This smouldering punk may be carried inside a bamboo tube. In another bamboo tube, carry moss gathered from the underside of tree limbs. From time to time, you should dry this moss out in the sun. Another method is that of filling a bamboo tube full of coals and ashes. These should last the day.

VI.

Foods from the Jungle, Beach and Sea

THERE is food to be had from these regions, although in many places it is not abundant. The chief difficulty lies in knowing where to find and how to recognise the food that does exist.

In order to increase your ability to recognise these foods, and your familiarity with what these regions afford, it would be wise to have a native living in the vicinity of your base point out the native foods to you, and show you how to prepare and preserve them should the necessity arise.

One good rule to follow is never to eat a red-colored vegetable unless you see a native doing so, nor to use water from vines which have a whitish sap.

FOODS FOUND IN THE JUNGLE

EDIBLE PALM (a variety of local names) : There is a short, squat, palm tree that can be identified by the black horsehair-like tendrils which surround the trunk. The tree is rarely more than 15 to 20 feet high, and it has a typical palm leaf. At a point approximately 4 feet above the ground, the main branches of the tree leave the trunk. The wood is soft and easily cut on the bias. A section approximately 2 feet long should be cut out of the trunk, just below the point where the main branches spread. This should be whittled down until nothing but the white, lustrous, soft centre is left. The texture of the wood is such that it is readily peeled off in circular sheathes which surround the soft, white interior. The latter looks like nothing so much as lobster meat. This soft, white interior can be eaten raw and has a delightful, clean, crisp taste.

SAGO PALM : The Sago Palm tree, usually 25 to 30 feet high, may be recognised by the leaf which has long thorns in the underside of the mid-rib. It is abundant in fresh-water swamps in the coastal regions.

- Sago is the main food of many natives. This food, prepared from the flour of the heart of the sago palm, looks, smells, and tastes like mucilage, and may be used for the same purposes as paste.

- The food may be used as it is received from the natives, but it is preferable to bake it for 25 to 30 minutes.

- Sticks of wild sugarcane or pineapple baked with it, will improve the taste considerably.

NIPA PALM : This palm closely resembles the young sago tree, but it is not thorned and does not develop a trunk or stem. It is commonly found in brackish water swamps along the tidal portions of streams. The white kernels of the fruit, the size of chestnuts, can be eaten raw as long as they are still soft and slimey. The tree may also be tapped as a water-substitute at this time. This sap is faintly sweet. This is a source of water in areas where the streams are brackish.

RATTAN SHOOTS (in Pidgin—"Kunda") : The spike of growth beyond the last two leaves is edible, either raw or cooked. The tiny spines should be cut off the spike and the balance boiled. The foot or base of the large vines (2½" in diameter), may be baked. The starchy material in the woody segments is edible.

FERNS (in Malay—"Pakoe") : There are some varieties of ferns, the tender and young leaves of which form a tasty green similar to spinach. The "Pakoe Sajor" is most suitable. This grows most usually in low, sandy places, along river-banks, and in marshy places.

Another variety is a stem fern which sometimes attains a height up to 7 feet. It has a strongly developed, erect rootstock, which often sticks out above the ground, and it is frequently covered thickly with long horse-hair-like, black roots, which slope downward or float upon the water. Its leaves are crowded together on the top. The white heart of the stem makes a very good vegetable. The young leaves and shoots can also be eaten, but the natives do not like them. It grows preferably on high ground, but it may be found also in the lowlands.

Other ferns with edible young leaves and shoots are : the Bird's Nest Fern ("Pakoe Pandan"), the "Pakoe Ramiding," which has lobster-red young leaves, and occurs much in swamp forest, on sandy soil, and, particularly, along the banks of rivers and brooks; and the "Pakoe Tikoes."

BAMBOO SHOOTS (in Malay—"Reboeng") : Bamboo shoots appear from near the base of the older stalks. This newly formed shoot will eventually become the bamboo stem. They resemble asparagus tips. Chop them into small pieces and either boil in water in a pan, or cook them in a fresh bamboo tube until the bamboo tube is nearly charred through.

KANKOENG : This is a water-plant and grows on inundated and marshy ground, preferably in fresh water. It also grows over the water, forming a dense, floating patch. The heart-shaped leaves are very nutritious and rich in vitamins.

WILD RASPBERRIES : These are found in the higher mountain regions. They have small, red, tart berries growing on erect or climbing shrubs or ground vines. The shrub may be from five to ten feet long.

PASSIFLORA : These are wild passion fruit, growing on spreading vines along the ground. When ripe, the fruit turns from light green to orange and is covered by a spidery whorl of soft green fuzz. The food is about the size of a large grape. The pulp is full of soft tomato-like seeds. The entire pulp, seeds and all, may be swallowed. It has a slightly tart but refreshing taste.

BREADFRUIT : This is the fruit of a most common tree which grows to a height of 50 to 60 feet. The fruit is a dark green oval with a rough skin. It resembles a melon, approximately 7 inches long by 4 or 5 inches in diameter. The leaves of the tree are glossy green and look like a hand with many fingers. When the fruit is ripe, it will drop off the tree and squash on the ground. This will expose a large number of chestnut-like kernels, which are in the interior of the variety with seeds. These seeds are the edible portion of this variety, and should be roasted in the ashes. They taste not unlike roasted chestnuts. The seedless variety should be cooked by baking the whole fruit in the coals of a fire. The interior then may be scooped out and eaten, the taste being similar to boiled potato.

WILD GINGER (In Pidgin — "Goragora") : This is a bush with slender, reed-like stalks from which long, narrow, green leaves grow directly. A separate stalk should be pulled up from the ground and there will be found at the roots, white, conical-shaped protuberances which are the new shoots. These can be eaten raw and have a taste slightly similar to commercial ginger.

NEW GUINEA CABBAGE (In Pidgin — "Kanangoro") : The most common source of greens throughout New Guinea is the young leaf of a small tree or bush which grows to a height of approximately 5 feet. The leaves are 2 to 4 inches long and the young ones are characterized by a smooth, glossy green colour. The leaves can be eaten raw, but make a very good spinach when chopped up and boiled.

BANANAS : Take green bananas and bake them until the skins are charred. The kinds found near the coast ("Pisang Radja" or "Pisang Ambon") are very good. Plantains are a type of small hard bananas which must be baked or boiled before they are edible.

FRUITS AND BERRIES : If the birds or monkeys eat them, they're probably safe for you.

DJEROOK BALI : A Malay word for a large citrus fruit, about the size of a grape fruit. It is very good and may safely be eaten raw. The word "Muli" applies to all citrus fruits in Pidgin English.

PAW PAW : This is an orange or yellow fruit which grows on a small tree, 15 to 20 feet high. The fruit projects from around the trunk, just under the lowest branches. It may be eaten raw. There Is an erroneous' belief that the black seeds of this fruit will protect you from malaria.

WILD PINEAPPLE : These are small and scarce, but very tasty. They may be eaten raw, If the hands and knife are clean. Otherwise, you should boil them.

COCONUTS : These grow abundantly in the coastal areas. Those which are found inland usually do not produce fruit. The meat inside the shell is good food. In order to get it out, place a sharpened stick or machete in the ground, and remove the husk by bringing it down on this implement. Having removed the husk, then bring the eye of the nut down hard on the implement. The meat is easily chipped loose with your knife blade, or chew it off the inner shell. The coconut milk is a fine substitute for water. Use green, fully grown and nearly matured nuts. The milk from the fallen nut is not so tasty. You can also use the nuts as canteens. If the husk is not removed, the milk will keep for about a week; if the husk has been taken off, the milk will remain for only a few days. (Again, the milk from the fallen nut will keep longer but will not taste as good). You can also pour water into nuts from which you have drained the milk and use them as spare water bottles. Some of the meat will dissolve, but it is not harmful. You can make coconut oil for frying or basting meat by cracking the shell of a nut, scraping the meat off in a creamy mass, placing it in another coconut shell, and allowing it to dry in the sun. The residue will be an opaque, oily fluid. Don't use it on metals or leather, as it will corrode the former and rot the latter.

PANDANUS NUTS : The Pandanus Palm is recognised easily. It looks as if it were growing in a series of stilt-like roots. It is quite abundant in the swampy areas of New Guinea and the islands to the east. Its fruit resembles a pineapple in shape, size and color. It has a segmented surface, and the soft, sweet, juicy ends of the segments are edible. The softer parts of the segments may be scraped off and formed into a cake. This in turn may either be dried in the sun or rolled into banana leaves, or stuffed into a bamboo tube and baked. The baked cake can be carried along on trips as an emergency ration. The nut is found in the outer part of the segment and may be eaten when mashed and cooked for about half an hour.

JAVA ALMOND : This is found in the jungles of the N.E.I. The fruits from this tall tree are round or oblong. The entire space in the nut is taken up by one or more kernels. The ripe fruits are black in color and the white kernels resemble almonds in ap-. pearance and taste. In the N.E.I. jungle, there are also numerous other edible fruits.

WILD YAMS : The wild yam is used by the natives at times when their food supplies are low. There are often twenty or thirty large, grey tubers with thorny fibres through them. Unless prepared properly, they are poisonous, and the sap will cause a skin rash. The fresh tubers should be peeled, cut into thin slices and left in salt water for a day. They are then kneaded and washed in fresh water, until the water ceases to turn white, after which they are dried in the sun and later boiled.

FOODS FOUND IN NATIVE GARDENS

The common vegetables are scarce in the jungles and seldom occur outside the natives' gardens. They do not occur in the heavily timbered portion, and in the other parts they are difficult to find among the mass of vegetation.

TARO (in Malay—"Kelasi" or "Talas") : The edible part is the large tuberous root, closely resembling a potato. It is one of the main foods of the natives of the South and South-west Pacific Areas. The leaves of these plants are large, dark-green, and look very similar to the canna.

The whole tuber should be put into the fire and let cook for about an hour. Then cut off the charred outside and eat the centre part. It may be sliced thinly similar to potato chips, or in finger-like French fries, and fried in coconut oil.

YAMS (in Malay—"Batatas"; in Pidgin—"Kau Kau") : The yam is very similar to sweet potato and may be prepared in the same manner. The leaves are three-pointed, and occasionally have a brown spotted tinge. The vines are found around the clearings or areas of secondary growth.

SPINACH : Substitutes are available from several sources:—

- **Kong Kong, Seior, Aibika** or **Kumu** are the various names for the native spinach.

- **Bajam** is an Indies spinach which has a spiny leaf. It is a very nourishing, and a savoury vegetable.

- **Laboe Melon** leaves or the leaves of the yam are edible.

TAPIOCA OR CASSAVE (in Malay—"Oebi Kajoe"; in Pidgin—"Maniok") : This is a shrub seven to ten feet high, with 3 to 7 segments. The edible part is the tuberous root. This must be cooked by roasting or boiling. It is poisonous if eaten raw. To boil the root:—Peel, wash and boil for 15 minutes; then re-boil them in fresh water until done. These may be rolled into glowing coals. The leaves may be eaten if par-boiled through several waters. The plants occur in gardens or along sandy stream banks in their wild state.

PINEAPPLES, PAW PAWS, CUCUMBERS, TOMA-TOES, MAIZE AND POTATOES : These, too, may be found in native gardens.

SUGAR CANE (in Malay—"Teboe") : This cane is similar to the cultivated type except it is not as large nor as sweet as the domestic species. Chewing sugar cane while on the trail will save the water supply.

MELON : In Dutch New Guinea, termed "Laboe," it closely resembles the pumpkin.

MEATS

FROGS : Tree frogs are relatively abundant. They and ground frogs present a very good and rather sus-taining diet. The legs are the edible portion. In order to destroy the parasites which may occur in the leg muscles, it is necessary to cook them. These may be boiled or fried in coconut oil, or grilled on a spit. The tree frog may be caught by slapping it with a switch, but to catch the ground variety, do so either by gigging or by splitting the last two feet of a long bamboo pole which is used to slap and stun the frog.

BATS : The large species is called "Flying Fox" or "Black Boxis," and has a body about the size of that of a large cat. They are night-feeders, and are commonly found in the tops of coconut palms. During, the day, they usually nest in the Nipa Palm Groves. They may be caught either by slapping them down or by shooting. As soon as possible after they are caught, the musk sacks under their fore-legs must be removed or the meat will have a tainted favour. The meat may be boiled, baked, grilled or fried.

CROCODILES : Their meat is not very palatable. However, the natives eat it and may offer some to you. It is best to par-boil it through several waters and then fry it in coconut oil or you might grill it, simultaneously basting it with coconut oil. The heart, the liver, and the steaks around the tail muscles are the edible portions.

LAND SNAILS : There are several varieties of the land snail that may be found in the jungle. Only the foot should be eaten, and this should be pounded well before boiling or grilling.

RATS AND BANDICOOTS : The latter resembles a rat, but has long hind legs like a kangaroo. The natives use both for food.

JUNGLE FOWL, WILD DUCK, PIGEONS, COVES, COCKATOOS, HORNBILL, CASSAWARIES, AND OTHER WILD BIRDS : These may be found in varying degrees of abundance in different parts of the jungle. They should be boiled, grilled or baked. Cassawaries are found in the Indies only on the Aroe Islands, Dutch New Guinea, and Salawati.

WILD FOWL EGGS : These will be found in nests which are heaps of leaves and twigs, three to four feet high.

WILD PIGS : But be sure that they are wild pigs, as the natives prize their domesticated pigs highly. These are identified by a slit in the ear. In the Netherland East Indies pigs are abundant and many roam the jungle.

LARGE LIZARDS : These are about two feet long. When disturbed, they will run a short distance and climb partly up a tree, pause on the far side, where they may be stalked and shot. The flesh, which resembles the white meat of chicken, should be boiled, grilled, baked or fried.

KANGAROOS : The hind legs of the small jungle kangaroo, and the heart and liver, make good meat. This meat from the leg should be prepared by boiling it for about 4 hours or by packing it in mud and baking it, or by grilling.

CUSCUS : This is a furry-tailed, reddish brown or grey-to-white possum. Its meat is very greasy and must either be boiled or grilled. These animals are difficult to see in the trees and equally difficult to get out of the tree when shot.

DEER : Several species of deer are found in the Indies, except on the Aroe Islands or to the eastward. They are to be found grazing in the savannahs in the evenings.

FRESH WATER FISH AND SHELL FISH

FRESH WATER FISH : All fresh water fish must be cooked. They contain injurious intestinal parasites which cooking will destroy. The most common fresh water fish is the Catfish, but even those are not abundant, except in the larger muddy rivers.

FRESH WATER SHELL FISH : Crawfish and Shrimps are to be found in lakes; deep holes in the river mud flats. They may be caught in dip-nets, made of woven palm leaves and twigs. Place the net behind the fish and poke a stick at them—they usually will back into the net. Or, place a bait of meat in the net, lower it into the water for a few minutes, then, quickly raise it. You must cook your catch in boiling water, or roast them in the coals. Mussels are fresh water clams which usually are to be found along streams, on large gravel or sand-bars. Prepare them by steaming them in their shells.

SEA FOOD

TURTLE EGGS : These may be found by following the turtle's clearly defined double trail in the sand for about twenty yards from the water to the nest. The eggs, which do not harden with cooking, should be boiled for at least 10 minutes.

TURTLE MEAT : Some turtles have a poison-bag under the neck, which must be removed. The meat under the shell of the back may be boiled. Small turtles may be dropped bodily into boiling water and cooked for twenty minutes.

MARINE SHELL FISH : There are various types of shell fish that may be found near the sea. Crawfish, lobsters and crabs may be caught in dip-nets at ebb tide when they are exposed on the surface or hidden under rocks. Their flesh may be eaten raw, provided they are salt water and not fresh water fish, but it will taste better if cooked. The large, black Mangrove Crab makes the choicest eating. It is found on mud flats on the seaward side of mangrove jungles, and can be easily killed with a stick. Its meat must be cooked in boiling water. Clams will provide you with a nutritious juice that may be used as a thirst quencher. Prepare the clams by steaming them in their shells.

Do not eat cone-type shell fish (varieties of snails), as they are poisonous. You will recognise them because an opening extends the entire length of the shell, and the shell is covered with white or buff spots.

MARINE FISH : Practically all salt water fish are free of parasites and may be eaten raw. There is an abundant food supply in the reefs along the coast. At night, certain varieties swim close to the shore in tha shallow water, or you may attract them by using a bark flare or flash-light. You can also catch them by hitting them with sticks or by spearing. Make your spear by lashing three sharpened sticks (each about one foot long) to a nine-foot stick. Fig tree bark, parachute ropes, or vines may be used for lashing. When spearing fish, aim below the visual object, as the water reflection causes the fish to appear nearer to the surface than it actually is.

Eat the fish raw or the flesh may be cut into narrow strips and dried in the sun. You may then cook it when and as desired. A few fish are poisonous, but any normal looking fish is edible. Those that are covered with spines, are not worth wasting time with anyway.

EELS make very good eating. Catch them either with a hook-and-line, or by using a noose on the end of a long pole. Further back on the pole, place another cord with a piece of bait. As the eel moves toward the bait, it can be snared in the noose. You must boil, grill or bake the meat. Eels may be distinguished from Sea Snakes (which are poisonous), by their manner of movement. Eels move easily and more gracefully through the water, while the snake swims with a wriggling motion, which is similar to the manner of movement of a land snake. Also, the eel does not have the body covering of boney plates or scales like the sea snake.

HOW TO STEW VEGETABLES

Dig a hole about two feet in diameter and one foot deep. Line it with large leaves, permitting them to stick out over the edges of the hole. Then, pile into the hole the edible leaves, palmite, bamboo shoots, etc. Heat a good many large stones in a fire. When they are thoroughly hot, wrap them in leaves and push them into the pile of vegetables in the hole. Cover the pile with the ends of the lining leaves which you had left projecting and fix this lid in place with a heavy stone or piece of wood. In forty to sixty minutes your meal will be nicely done.

Tubers can be cooked in the same way, mixed with leaves. You can also toast them like chestnuts in hot ashes.

PRESERVATION OF FOOD SUPPLY

All food must be protected from ants and flies. The latter are not only most numerous but are the car-riers of amoebic dysentery.

- Surplus food may be stored in bamboo tubes, with a plug made of a slightly smaller bamboo.

- Extra supplies of fish and meat may be preserved by "jerking." Cut the flesh into thin strips, wash it in salt water, and hang it in the sun to dry.

ROASTING STICK

COCONUT HUSKER

BILLY CAN

VI.

First Aid

MALARIA : The only way you can get malaria is from the bite of an infected mosquito. To prevent infection, you must keep your body covered with clothing through which the mosquito cannot bite. You can, and should, if you have it, take medicine as a suppressive. If you have Atabrine Tablets, take one tablet daily. If you get an attack of fever, increase the doseage to three tablets for six or seven successive days. If you have Quinine rather than Atabrine, take one five-grain tablet each morning and one each evening. In the event of an attack, increase the doseage to six a day for five days.

BURNS AND SUNBURN : Apply antiseptic, such as Sulfadiazine ointment, but not Iodine.

RINGWORM : This is a common jungle infection, and little need be done for it until you return, when it can be easily cured with medication. Iodine will help to prevent infection.

DYSENTERY : This can be avoided if you cook all foods and boil or purify all water. Any foods that may be eaten raw, must be handled with clean hands. Carry some Sulfaguanidine Tablets in your jungle kit, and take according to directions until the diarrhoea ceases.

BITES, CUTS, SCRATCHES, BREAKS IN THE SKIN : You must treat these promptly to prevent the formation of tropical ulcers. Whenever the skin is broken, dab on Mercurochrome, Sulfanilamide Powder or other antiseptic. Then cover with adhesive tape. Leave the tape on unless the skin becomes inflamed. (Iodine is not recommended, for it may cause a burn.)

SNAKE BITES : These are rare, but, if you do get one, quickly apply a tourniquet above the wound (use the shroud line from your 'chute or a vine). Then wash or lick the skin at the bite to remove the venom on the surface. Make an incision crosswise through the fang marks, to the depth of half an inch. Suck the wound. Loosen the ligature for 15 seconds every 20 minutes and remove completely after two hours. Dust on some Sulfanilamide Powder and put on a bandage. Leave the bandage on unless the skin becomes inflamed.

LEECH BITES : When the leech bites you it injects a substance which prevents your blood from coagulating. Hence, the wound will continue to bleed for some minutes. The wound easily becomes infected and causes a tropical ulcer. Immediately remove the leech by touching it with a drop of iodine, a lit cigarette, or by a steady, gentle pull. (If you jerk it out, the teeth will remain inside the wound, causing infection). After removal, the wound should be squeezed until it stops bleeding, then it must be sterilised and bandaged.

SCORPIONS AND CENTIPEDES : The bites of these animals are painful, but not fatal. There is little likelihood of your being bitten unless you sleep on the bare ground or pick up rocks without first kicking them over. No treatment is necessary for these bites, but do not scratch them or you will infect them and cause ulcers.

BITES OF FLIES, ANTS AND TICKS : They are more of a nuisance than a source of danger. Don't scratch their bites or you will infect them. Ticks may be removed by a drop of iodine or scraped off with a knife blade. The wound should be treated similarly to a leech bite.

DANGEROUS ANIMALS

CROCODILES : The crocodile is the most dangerous animal found in these regions. It is neither cowardly, nor afraid of man, and its actions are the more dangerous because unpredictable. One time, a crocodile may quietly slide away from you; the next, it may attack you or your canoe. They inhabit most stream courses, particularly those with muddy banks, the stagnant courses and the river swamp areas associated with the larger streams. They are also to be found in lakes and along the swampy borders of lakes.

If attacked by a crocodile, jab your thumbs into the eyes. If in a rubber dinghy, where there are crocodiles about, one method which may successfully keep them at bay is to keep tapping the metal oar. The Dyaks of Borneo use this method with success when paddling their canoes. Usually each paddler will knock his paddle against the side of the canoe with each stroke, while one of the party will keep up a constant tapping on the bottom of the boat.

PIGS AND CASSAWARIES : They may attack if disturbed when in company of their young or when wounded.

KARABAU : There large, slow-moving water buffalo of the Indies and the Philippines are dangerous to the white man, even when domesticated. It is not advised that a novice attempt to kill one for food.

SNAKES : Snakes are not abundant, and are seldom seen. In some localities, snakes are unknown. Many of the snakes are poisonous, including some with the small round-type head.

VIII

Survival at Sea

THE most important factor in survival at sea is the advance preparation. Your equipment should be complete, and you should have a thorough knowledge of its use. Your chances then of being picked up are greater, and you will save yourself many uncomfortable hours in the water.

BEFORE TAKING OFF ON A MISSION

Inspect your life-raft kit previous to each mission. Grease your knife, Very pistol and automatic before every long over-water flight. Place flares, first-aid kit, and any other pieces you feel may be ruined by salt water, in waterproof bags.

Check your Mae West; be sure that the CO_2 bottles are filled and unpunctured.

SEA CRASH

It is impossible to guess with accuracy how long your plane will remain afloat, due to the many factors which must be taken into consideration. Usually it will remain afloat for at least a few minutes, giving you time to release your life raft.

● If you are a fighter pilot, release your canopy before the plane touches the water.

● Pull inflation cords and hold on to the tow-rope as the raft is thrown free of the plane. This will prevent the raft from floating beyond your reach by the actions of the wind and sea.

● Should the raft inflate in an upside-down position, you can right it by lying across it and lifting the side towards the wind. The wind will thus help you turn it over. While you are doing this, hold on to the tow-rope to prevent the wind from blowing the raft beyond your reach.

● All equipment when not in use should be kept in the side pockets of the raft to prevent it from being washed overboard.

● Do not walk around inside the raft with your shoes on. Remove, but keep them, for they will be needed should you reach shore before being rescued. Keep your socks on to protect your feet from sunburn and to reduce the effect of the salt water on them.

● At least for the first few days, and until your body has gradually become accustomed to the sun, keep covered under the poncho between the hours of 1000 and 1500.

The time for sending out your S.O.S. messages on the radio included in the large raft equipment is 15 minutes before and after the hour.

SOURCES OF WATER AT SEA

There are tins of water aboard the raft.

Rainwater may be gathered, during squalls, in the poncho; you can also catch rainwater in your clothes. It is necessary to rinse out the clothing in the first rain in order to rid the garments of the salt which will have accumulated in them from the spray. Slightly brackish water is not injurious to the system.

A water substitute may be obtained by dicing fish flesh, placing it in a shirt sleeve or some other cloth, and wringing out the juice.

Fish blood, the blood of sea birds, and chewing raw fish flesh, will help quench thirst.

SOURCES OF FOOD AT SEA

Food rations are aboard the raft.

Fish may be caught by using the fishing kit in-cluded in the raft's equipment, by shooting, or attract-

ing flying-fish into the boat at night with your flash-
light.

Sea birds may be shot.

IN ENEMY-PATROLLED WATERS

The poncho, attached to the oar, may be used as
a sail.

Keep the oar (mast) under the poncho so that no
reflected gleam of the sun will disclose your presence.

If any enemy plane is sighted, drape the poncho,
with the blue-green camouflage side up, over as much
of the raft as possible.

Be prepared to reverse the poncho, yellow side up,
if a friendly plane is sighted.

If an enemy plane approaches you, go over the
side, hold on to the tow-rope and duck under the water
when the plane comes within strafing range.

Should there be any bullet holes in your raft, use
the wooden screw plugs to seal them.

IN FRIENDLY-PATROLLED WATERS

The orange-yellow side of the poncho should be toward the sky.

Your signalling equipment—mirror, sea marker, Very pistol, flashlight, etc., should be handy at all times for signalling an approaching friendly plane.

BAILING OUT INTO THE SEA

Should you bail out at sea or should your plane sink too rapidly for you to recover the raft, you will be dependent on your Mae West, which, if in proper condition, can keep you afloat indefinitely.

● Rid yourself of your 'chute, if possible, just before you strike the water.

● Do not inflate the Mae West until you are in the water.

● If the CO_2 tubes fail to inflate it, use the manual tube. If this, too, fails (because the Mae West has been punctured), you can use your 8.2 Chino shirt as an emergency life preserver; button the shirt around the neck and waist; then exhale air into the open front side. This will inflate the back part of the shirt and it will retain the air for an hour or more. Repeat the process when it has become deflated. The Chino trousers, with the legs knotted, can be used similarly.

● If there is no land in sight, discard your shoes.

IX

Survival on Low, Sandy Islands

THROUGHOUT the South Pacific and South-west Pacific areas there are numerous, low, sandy, coralline islands. Topographically, they rise from the sandy beaches to an elevation of thirty-five to forty feet, from which point they slope inward towards a central basin. This may or may not include a salt water lagoon.

Water and food sources, and protection from the sun, offer your biggest problems if force-landed on these atolls. Survivors on islands, however, can be more easily seen and picked up by search planes or boats, particularly if they are fortunate to have signalling equipment (mirror, flares, dinghy, etc.).

WATER

On some of the larger of the islands, wells can be found which will yield a brackish water. These wells are shallow, for the fresh water is close to the surface and the salt water directly below.

Rain water is another source. If you have no water bottle or canteen, you can collect and store this water in coconut shells and in the lungs of your Mae West.

Water will usually be found by digging a hole near the inner slope (near the central basin or lagoon) to a depth of three to five feet. If no water is found there, then a hole above high water mark on the beach should be tried as previously mentioned.

Your body will absorb a certain amount of water by resting an hour or two each day in the sea.

The juice squeezed from diced fish flesh, and the blood of fish and sea birds will help augment your supply, as will the milk from coconuts.

FOOD

Fish, shell fish (except cone and spindle shaped), and coconuts will form the chief sources of your diet on these islands, unless they are inhabited. In such a case, vegetables can be obtained from the natives and their gardens. Never eat fish which have slimy gills, sunken eyes, flabby flesh or skin, an unpleasant odor, or fish with bristles instead of the usual scales.

PROTECTION FROM THE SUN

On most of the islands in the tropics, some protection from the sun is necessary to prevent sunstroke and sunburn, particularly if you lack normal clothing or equipment from which to make an overhead protective covering.

You can make yourself a hat of leaves.

A shelter can be made from branches, palm leaves, or other vegetation.

A substitute for shoes can be made from coconut husks, and you can cover the tops of your feet with leaves to prevent burning.

Another idea is to bury your body in the damp sand during the hottest hours of the day.

SIGNALLING TO RESCUE PLANES

Make use of all the methods set forth previously in this booklet. Keep piles of dry wood in readiness for use. Another suggestion is to put on your Mae West and get into the water. The contrast of the yellow Mae West and the water is fairly striking. And last, but not least, the signalling mirror offers one of the best means of attracting attention.

PHYSIC NUT – POISONOUS SHRUB
(10' TO 15')

COWHAGE – POISONOUS VINE

MANZANILLO-TREE

AVOID

TREE NETTLE, STINGING SHRUB

75

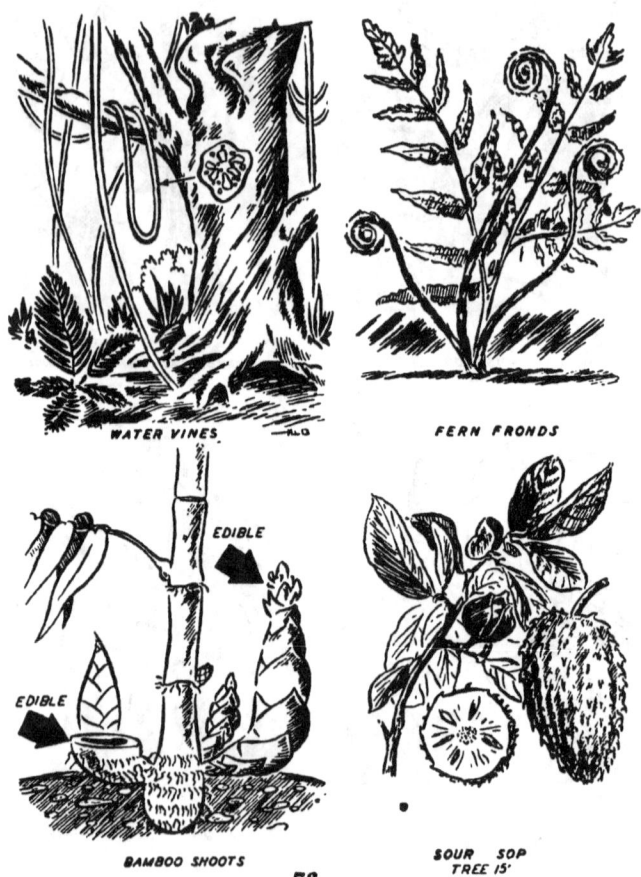

WATER VINES

FERN FRONDS

EDIBLE

EDIBLE

BAMBOO SHOOTS

SOUR SOP
TREE 15'

76

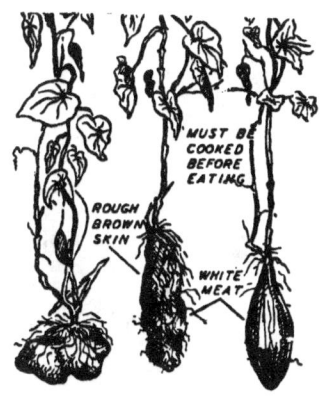

MUST BE
COOKED
BEFORE
EATING

ROUGH
BROWN
SKIN

WHITE
MEAT

YAM -
LOW OR CLIMBING VINE

RAW OR ROASTED

INDIAN ALMOND - LARGE TREE

PURSLANE - LOW FLESHY WEED

YOUNG SHOOTS
& TUBERS
EDIBLE WHEN
THOROUGHLY
COOKED -

TARO (1½ FT)

77

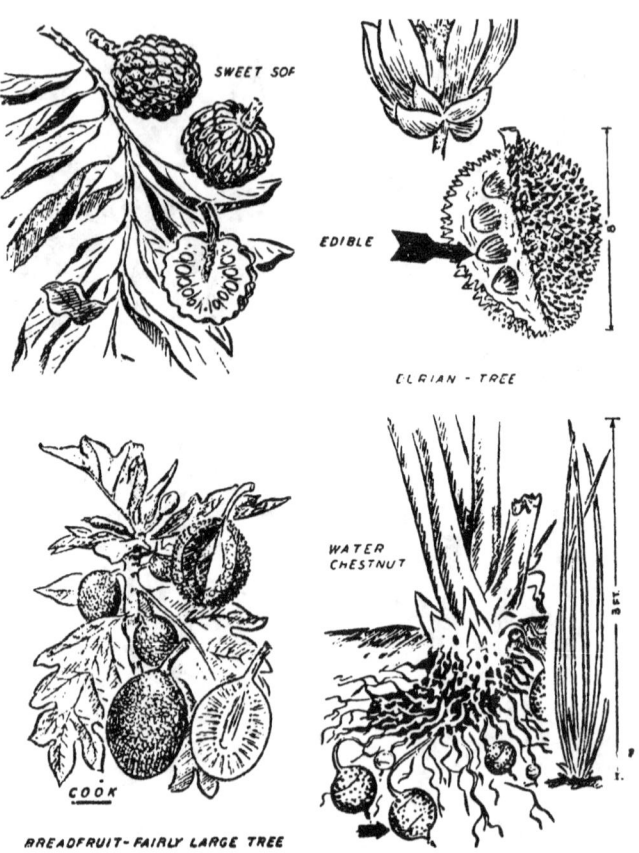

SWEET SOF

EDIBLE

ELRIAN - TREE

WATER CHESTNUT

COOK

BREADFRUIT-FAIRLY LARGE TREE

78

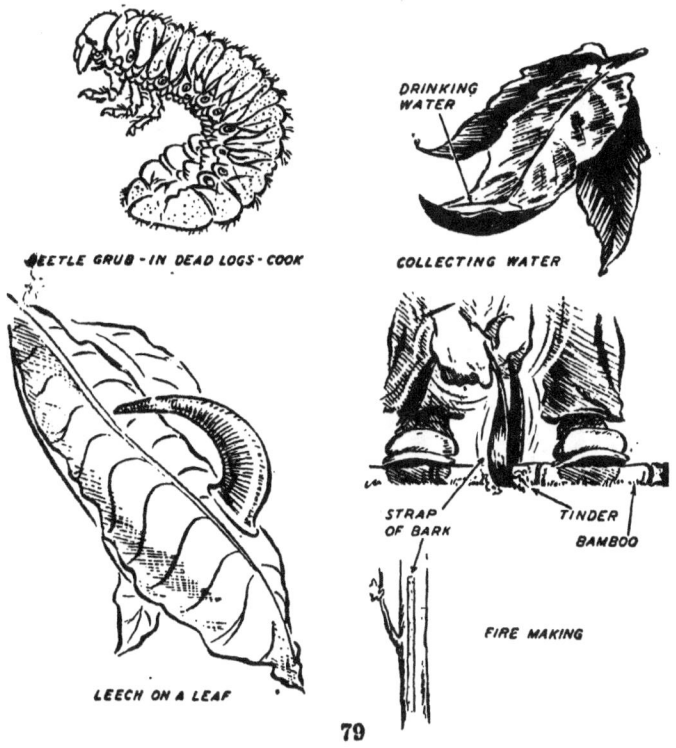

BEETLE GRUB - IN DEAD LOGS - COOK

DRINKING
WATER

COLLECTING WATER

LEECH ON A LEAF

STRAP
OF BARK

TINDER

BAMBOO

FIRE MAKING

79

www.ingramcontent.com/pod-product-compliance
Lightning Source LLC
Chambersburg PA
CBHW070400290526
45790CB00004B/1580